MY FIRST BOOK
ZIMBABWE

ALL ABOUT ZIMBABWE FOR KIDS

GLOBED
CHILDREN BOOKS

Interior and cover Design: Daniel Day
Editor: Margaret Bam

For My Sons, Daniel, David and Jude

Great Zimbabwe Ruins, Zimbabwe

Zimbabwe

Zimbabwe is a **country**.

A country is land that is controlled by a **single government**. Countries are also called **nations, states, or nation-states**.

Countries can be **different sizes**. Some countries are big and others are small.

Great Zimbabwe National Monument, Zimbabwe

Where Is Zimbabwe?

Zimbabwe is located in the continent of Africa.

A continent is **a massive area of land that is separated from others by water or other natural features**.

Zimbabwe is situated in **Southern Africa.**

Harare, Zimbabwe

Capital

The capital of Zimbabwe is Harare.

Harare is located in the **Northern part** of the country.

Harare is the largest city in Zimbabwe.

Hwange National Park, Main Camp, Zimbabwe

Provinces

Zimbabwe is divided into eight provinces

The provinces of Zimbabwe are as follows:

1. **Mashonaland Central**
2. **Mashonaland East**
3. **Mashonaland West**
4. **Manicaland**
5. **Midlands**
6. **Masvingo**
7. **Matabeleland North**
8. **Matabeleland South**

Harare, Zimbabwe

Population

Zimbabwe has population of around **15.1 million people** making it the 73rd most populated country in the world.

Nyanga, Zimbabwe

Size

Zimbabwe is **390,757 square kilometres** making it the 73rd largest country in the world.

Zimbabwe is known for its picturesque landscapes, rugged terrain, rich biodiversity, abundant wildlife and diverse flora and fauna.

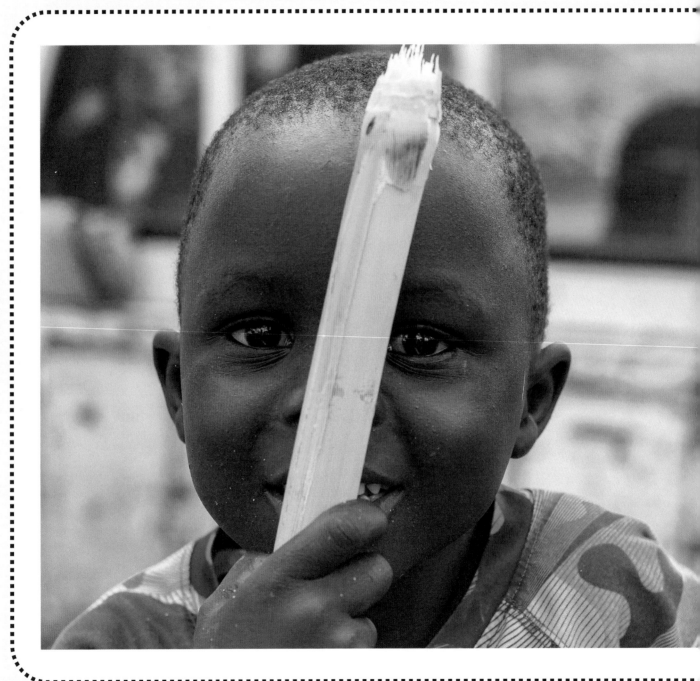

Languages

The official languages of Zimbabwe are **Chibarwe, English, Kalanga, Koisan, Nambya, Ndau, Ndebele, Shangani, Shona, sign language, Sotho, Tonga, Tswana, Venda, Xhosa and Chewa.**

Shona is the most widely spoken language in the country and is used by around 70 percent of the country.

Here are a few phrases in Shona
- **Hello - Hesi**
- **Sorry - Ndine urombo**
- **Thanks - Waita hako**

Victoria Falls, Zimbabwe

Attractions

There are lots of interesting places to see in Zimbabwe.

Some beautiful places to visit in Zimbabwe are

- **Victoria Falls**
- **Chinhoyi Caves**
- **Matusadona National Park**
- **Lake Kariba**
- **Victoria Falls National Park**

Nyanga, Zimbabwe

History of Zimbabwe

Zimbabwe has a long and fascinating history. The area has been home to various indigenous tribes such as the Shona and Ndebele people. These tribes established powerful kingdoms, including the Great Zimbabwe Kingdom, which flourished from the 11th to 15th centuries and was known for its impressive stone structures.

Zimbabwe gained independence from Britain in 1980.

Customs in Zimbabwe

Zimbabwe has many fascinating customs and traditions.

- Zimbabwe has a rich cultural heritage of traditional music and dance, with its own unique styles and instruments. The mbira is a popular musical instrument in Zimbabwe and is often used in traditional ceremonies and cultural performances.
- In Zimbabwean culture, respecting and honouring elders is highly valued. Younger generations are expected to show respect to their elders through gestures such as bowing.

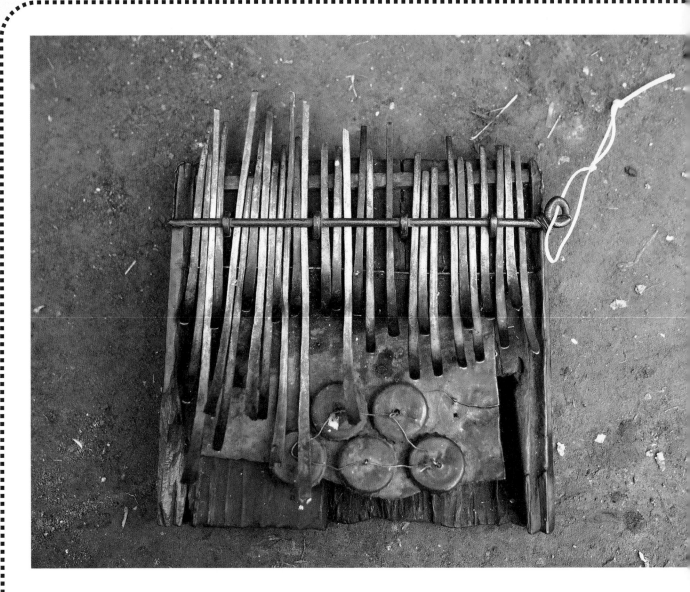

Mbira, Zimbabwean musical instrument

Music of Zimbabwe

There are many different music genres in Zimbabwe such as **Chimurenga, Afro-Jazz, Zimdancehall and Sungura.**

Some notable Zimbabwean musicians include
- **Jah Prayzah - A Zimbabwean contemporary musician and lead member of the band Third Generation.**
- **Berita - A Zimbabwean-born singer, songwriter and music producer.**

Sadza with vegetables and guinea fowl

Food of Zimbabwe

Zimbabwe is known for having delicious, flavoursome and rich dishes.

The national dish of Zimbabwe is **Sadza** which is a type of bread that is moulded using the hands to form balls.

Food of Zimbabwe

Zimbabwean cuisine is known for its hearty and flavourful dishes, often featuring staples such as cornmeal, meat, vegetables, and various types of relishes.

Some popular dishes in Zimbabwe include

- **Dovi: This is a peanut butter stew made with chicken or beef, vegetables, and spices.**
- **Chingwa: This is a traditional Zimbabwean dish made with roasted or boiled corn.**
- **Nyama Dishes: Zimbabweans enjoy various meat dishes, including braai (barbecue) and Biltong.**

Lake Kariba, Zimbabwe

Weather in Zimbabwe

Zimbabwe has a **tropical climate** which means that Zimbabweans enjoy warm weather all year. Zimbabwe has two distinct seasons; dry season and a rainy season.

The rainy season in Zimbabwe generally occurs from November to March, with varying amounts of rainfall across different regions of the country. The dry season in Zimbabwe takes place from April to October, when rainfall is scarce, and the weather is hot and dry.

Elephant in Zimbabwe

Animals of Zimbabwe

There are many wonderful animals in Zimbabwe.

Here are some animals that live in Zimbabwe

- **Elephants**
- **Lions**
- **Leopards**
- **Buffalo**
- **Rhinoceros**
- **Cheetahs**
- **Antelopes**

Gonarezhou National Park

National Parks

There are many beautiful National Parks in Zimbabwe which is one of the reasons why so many people visit this beautiful country every year.

Here are some of Zimbabwe's National Parks

- **Hwange National Park**
- **Mana Pools National Park**
- **Gonarezhou National Park**
- **South Gonarezhou National Park**
- **Matobo National Park**

Zimbabwe football fan

Sports of Zimbabwe

Sports play an integral part in Zimbabwe culture. The most popular sport is **Football.**

Here are some of famous sportspeople from Zimbabwe

- **Kirsty Coventry - Swimming**
- **Cara Black - Tennis**
- **Tatenda Taibu - Cricket**
- **Andrew Pattison - Tennis**
- **Stansly Maponga - American Football**

Robert Mugabe

Famous

Many successful people hail from Zimbabwe.

Here are some notable Zimbabwean figures

- **Robert Mugabe - Politician**
- **Herbert Chitepo - Revolutionary**
- **Christopher Chetsanga - Scientist**
- **Simon Muzenda - Politician**
- **Danai Gurira - Actress**

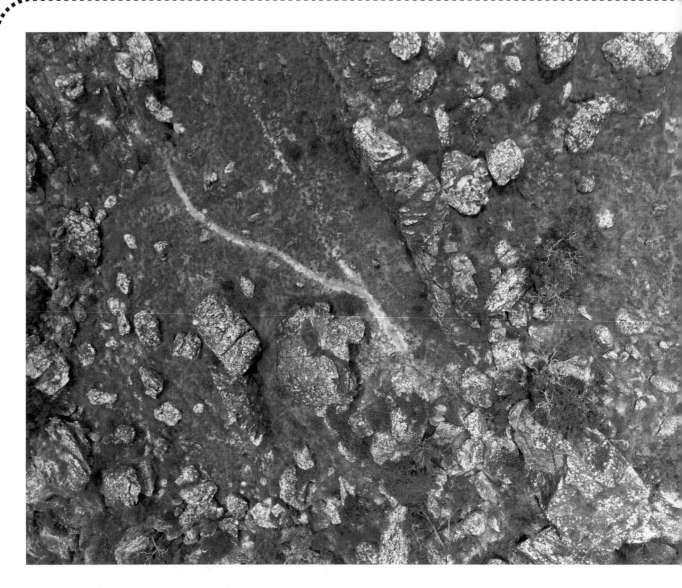

The Chimanimani Mountains

Something Extra...

As a little something extra, we are going to share some lesser known facts about Zimbabwe.

- Zimbabwe celebrates various festivals throughout the year, including cultural and traditional events such as the Harare International Festival of the Arts (HIFA), which is a showcase of music and dance.
- The Chimanimani Mountains are a stunning mountain range located in eastern Zimbabwe, near the border with Mozambique.

Words From the Author

We hope that you enjoyed learning about the wonderful country of Zimbabwe.

Zimbabwe is a country rich in culture and beauty, with lots of wonderful places to visit and people to meet.

We hope you continue to learn more about this wonderful nation. If you enjoyed this book, consider leaving a review!

With Love

Zimbabwe is

A country is land that is controlled by a group
Countries are also called

Countries can be   Some countries
are big and others are small

Interior text by Random Design Productions.

First Printing, 2023

When Bunford's friends come, he rushes downstairs

Printed in Great Britain
by Amazon

37041256R00027